Birthday Surprise

Written by Alison Hawes

Illustrated by Judy Brown

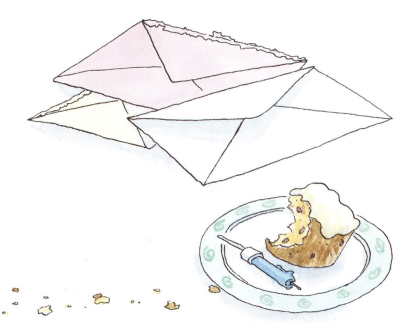

One day, we got up very early.

We made muffins.

My sister put in the milk.

I put in the egg.

My sister put in the fruit.

Dad put the muffins in the oven.

The muffins got bigger...

and bigger...

and bigger!

I put on the icing.

My sister put on the candles.

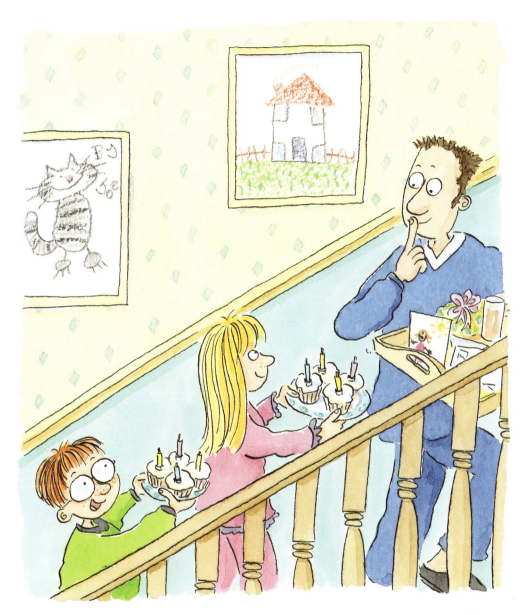